GRITTY. INDEPENDENT. RESOURCEFUL. LEADERS.

Sharon,

Thank you for telling the stories of people who lift each other up.

That's exactly what G.I.R.L.s do!

GRITTY. INDEPENDENT. RESOURCEFUL. LEADERS.

Jacqueline Cochran, Nancy Harkness-Love
and the Women Airforce Service Pilots

Written & Illustrated by
Robyn Itule

Before we take off into the blue yonder of history, let's chart our flight plan with a few important notes. This book is our aircraft, engineered to take you back in time to meet the incredible Women Airforce Service Pilots, the WASPs, of World War II.

As we fly through these pages, remember that we're navigating by the stars of actual events and true heroism. But, just like a skilled pilot adapts their maneuvers to the flying conditions, this story flies at an appropriate altitude for younger readers.

So, zip up your flight suit, put on your helmet, pull down those aviator goggles, and fasten your seatbelts for an adventure about courageous G.I.R.L.s and their feats of daring-do. Please remember that while this story is based on scholarly work, it's a simplified version of the facts and true stories.

This mission aims to inspire readers with the courage and determination of the WASPs, encouraging you to discover more about these and other gritty, independent, resourceful leaders of history.

Hopefully, this story is not your final destination, and you will take off on many more adventures to learn about gritty, independent, resourceful leaders from all over the world throughout history.

You've been cleared for take-off!

© 2024 by Robyn Itule.
All rights reserved. Unauthorized reproduction of this flight log is strictly prohibited without clearance from air traffic control.
ISBN: 9798880290789

For Mama Maj

In nineteen hundred forty-two, brave women took to the skies. These creative, bold, and gutsy gals helped their country and allies.

Each one of them was inspired to defend freedom and human rights. And they showed their love of country by rising to new heights.

On the ground, they worked hard with great passion and purpose. They fixed every kind of engine, wing, propeller, and circuit.

They crossed the country in airplanes, roaring louder than a riot. This is the high-flying tale of the Women Airforce Service Pilots.

They took off because of two remarkable women. They both wanted to make a difference using all the gifts they'd been given.

First, let's meet Jackie. A bold spirit determined to rise. A pioneer as a pilot, she was courage personified.

She didn't have much as a child but had soaring dreams. Jackie propelled herself toward her goals with great drive and self-esteem.

She trained as a beautician. She was an artist with makeup and hair. But while glossing lips and pinning curls, she daydreamed of being in the air.

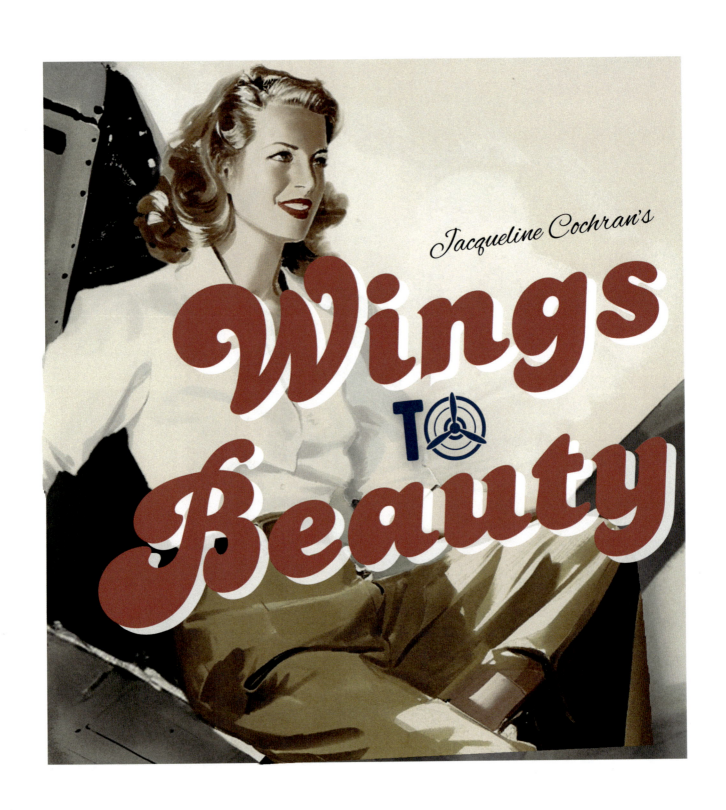

Jackie soon got her chance to take off and take flight. She dashed around the country. Top to bottom and left to right.

And why was she zooming from sea to shining sea? She was selling her own makeup brand named **Wings to Beauty**.

Jackie broke the mold for a woman in her time and place. Who says you can't be a fierce flyer and an expert at putting makeup on your face?

In a dress, flight suit, or uniform, Jackie made an impression on most folks for her style, patriotism, and the many barriers she broke.

Then there's Nancy Harkness Love - she adored aviation. She earned her pilot's license before her high school graduation!

In her first year at Vassar College, she was named **The Flying Freshman**. Nancy turned her passion into profit by flying friends home and back to school again.

Her father wanted to be sure she attended all her classes. But no one could stop Nancy from dreaming about soaring over rolling plains and mountain passes.

Nancy sure felt like she was flying when she met a man named Robert Love. They were a perfect match, like a pair of pilot gloves.

They built a business flying people and cargo places. And in her free time, Nancy competed in high-speed air races.

Every traveler can be grateful Nancy had no fear when asked to be the test pilot for a new landing gear.

She even tested new types of planes with different innovations. Nancy's testing helped set the bar for today's aviation.

In the early 1940s, the United States entered World War Two. To support U.S. soldiers and the Allied effort, these fearless female founders knew just what to do.

Jackie met with the First Lady, a woman named Eleanor, to propose a women's flying squadron who were ready to protect values worth fighting for.

At almost the same time, Nancy had an identical plan - to recruit an elite team of women pilots for the Army Air Corps Ferrying Command.

Fate was bringing them together. They were on the same crusade. Although they had important champions, there was more than one blockade.

Some said it wasn't right or thought women couldn't do it.
Some were just intimidated by their talent in the cockpit.

Jackie and Nancy knew their stuff - they'd flown millions of miles and meters. They also knew what G.I.R.L. stands for:

Gritty. Independent. Resourceful. Leader.

Some armed forces leaders knew this, too.
They said, "These **G.I.R.L.s** have great skill and heart!"

They gave Jackie and Nancy a mission: Recruit a team of women pilots ready to do their part.

So, Nancy and Jackie asked others to join the cause. Thousands of women applied to serve and fly without a moment's pause.

Together, they logged sixty million miles flying planes from factory to base. They repaired and tested aircraft to make sure every part was back in place.

Mission by mission, they proved with smarts and feats of daring-do when the stakes were high Women Airforce Service Pilots always saw it through.

These G.I.R.L.s with gumption earned respect on every base and post. They had a reputation as daredevils who don't boast.

After peace was finally won, what should happen then? Jackie and Nancy became the Women Airforce Service Pilots' champions.

Jackie kept on breaking records like the barrier of sound. She always saw the sky as her personal playground.

Nancy felt it was her duty to make sure proper thanks were paid to the Women Airforce Service Pilots for the contributions and sacrifices they made.

She told their story her whole life. Then in 1977, they were finally recognized as veterans, even those already in heaven.

Together, Nancy and Jackie and hundreds of fearless flying women, inspired others to go on all kinds of daring missions.

From Betty Miller's solo flight across the vast Pacific,
to the first female pilot to have a seat in a commercial airline cockpit.

Or the Arizona air base, where a first-of-its-kind class was made up of ten G.I.R.L.s who got their Silver Wings from the top brass.

Or the first woman Thunderbird, her aviation call sign was FiFi. On the ground, she's known by her rank, Air Force Colonel Nicole Malacowski.

If you ever need inspiration to go beyond and above,
look to the Women Airforce Service Pilots, Jacqueline Cochran and Nancy Harkness-Love.

Author's Note

This book came into being because the Women Airforce Service Pilots (WASP) are like a subplot to my life. Their story was told to me by my mom, and this book is my effort to hand it down to another generation.

My mom, Natalie J. Stewart-Smith, M.A., MEd, wrote her Master's thesis about the remarkable experiences and contributions of the Women Airforce Service Pilots. Titled: ***The Women Airforce Service Pilots (WASP) of World War II: Perspectives on the Work of America's First Military Women Aviators***, it was the first academic study of these incredible women. She defended her thesis in 1980 and received her Master's in history from Washington State University.

Second Lieutenant Stewart-Smith, 1972

I didn't always appreciate how extraordinary the research and WASP storytelling was. There are two reasons for that:

1. The content was ever-present for me from an early age. I had zero clue I was the only five-year-old who knew that Jacqueline Cochran was Amelia Erhart's friend.
2. Between the ages of 12 and 18, I was a typical tween/teenager who was unwavering in my dedication to be uninterested in anything my mom was interested in. (Sorry mom...I get it now...circle of life and all that.)

The first memory I have of the WASP is when I was in first grade. I won an art contest for a painting of Jaqueline Cochran and her plane. Sometimes, I imagine a youth art aficionado evaluating that masterpiece and considering it for inclusion in the Erie, Pennsylvania, Sister Cities art collection.

The author - with bangs inspired by Mary-Lou Retton - posing with her artwork.

Cocking their head to one side, they might have thought, "Perhaps the artist's use of pink demonstrates Jacqueline Cochran's boldness and joy at defying convention by embracing the feminine spirit in a male-dominated environment. Very deep. Profound even."

I can assure you the artist did not intend to imply any sub-context or sophisticated layered meaning communicated through color selections.

But yes, as it happens, that's precisely what Jacqueline Cochran did.

Around the same time, I vividly remember my mom's WASP friend Pat Pateman (Lt. Col., U.S.A.F., retired) visiting. She painted my nails for the first time. Bright red! My mom wasn't super happy she'd done that, and "Second Grandma Pat" put my mom in her place, reminding her that girls can do anything **and** wear nail polish while doing it. I couldn't believe how pretty my nails looked. And I really couldn't believe anyone could speak to my mom like without being sent to their room immediately!

My mom was active in several organizations where she ran in the same circle as our then-Congressman, Tom Ridge, and connected with women veterans like A. Jean Carson (C.O.L., Army Nurse Corps, retired). Following a presentation my mom gave, she was invited to attend the Vietnam Women Veterans Memorial groundbreaking.

I wrote a poem about what it would mean for women veterans to travel to Washington, D.C., to see the unveiling. A foreshadowing of this work? Perhaps! The poem was incorporated into a wreath representing Erie, Pennsylvania, displayed at the groundbreaking.

We attended the event, as evidenced by the photo at right -- which precisely captures the intensity of my awkward phase.

Oof! The Laura-Ashley-floral shirt and shorts set paired with a turquoise and fuchsia cross-body bag, round wireframe glasses, and, what appears to be an earnest (but failed) attempt at feathered bangs begs two questions:

What shoes did I complete this deeply tragic look with? Feels like lug sole sandals.

Left-to-right: Natalie Stewart-Smith, the author, A. Jean Carson, Pennsylvania Congressman Tom Ridge

And, why weren't all physical photo copies of this destroyed?!
Feels like a dark, nefarious and pre-meditated purpose, because it's been digitized!

If it wasn't already obvious, I'm taking my power back by proudly owning my awkward - which leads us to the next paragraph.

On another visit to our nation's capitol, we visited the Smithsonian Air and Space Museum, where a copy of my mom's thesis is preserved. This visit is memorable for me because:
- I made an Indiana Jones-esque escape from between two automated moving bookshelves. I just did not see that one coming, but I made it out alive.
- I got to eat astronaut ice cream. Calming after my high-adrenaline bookcase escape. Doesn't that sound like a Magic Tree House book title?
- I lost a purple glitter retainer* and my mom was not too pleased about it.

*See the above reference regarding the depths of my awkward stage, which persisted, and moved up a level to include orthodontia.

In 1996, my family moved from Pennsylvania to New Mexico. That was really tough for me, and I'm fairly certain my parents picked up on it.

I was awful company for all 1,765 miles of that road trip. If you look up the definition of "wallowing," you'll find picture of me with red, puffy eyes and an over-the-top sulk. What you can't see, is that I was listening to Wilson Phillips' song "Goodbye, Carmen" on repeat. This 90's deep cut features the lyrics "Hasta manana or who knows when? It all depends. Goodbye." Clearly, the dream was not still alive for me as we headed west.

The route took us through Sweetwater, Texas, so we could visit the Women Airforce Service Pilots Museum. I pouted the entire visit. (Sorry mom and dad.)

On the bright side, I never once sang the Goodbye Carmen lyrics aloud while we were in the company of others. Silver lining?

The good people who ran the museum graciously ignored me and happily accepted a copy of my mom's work to keep as part of the official collection.

Natalie Stewart-Smith and Steve Smith at a NMMI event. Probably opening night of Antigone. Side Note: Agamemnon is the actual worst!

Once we were settled in New Mexico, my mom became an English professor at New Mexico Military Institute (NMMI) and taught for the better part of two decades. In addition to the lessons of correct grammar and how to properly shine boots she taught a generation of cadets that compassion is the foundation of leadership, and she led by example.

She also taught theater!

These lessons included the real-life importance of annunciation when delivering lines like "the pilot of the ship." (If you say it five times fast, you'll hear it.) Less relevant today, but no less important, she taught them handy verbal tools like Shakespearean insult hurling.

Fun fact: My son (age nine at the time of publication) only had to say "the pilot of the ship" three times fast to achieve the amusing result. My husband and I are mature and responsible parents so we laughed about it in another room.

More recently, my mom is a sought-after speaker about women in aviation. She travels and gives presentations about the WASP and the Women's Army Corps. When I've attended events with her, she's the woman others want to meet and a person they're eager to collaborate or make plans with.

The author and her mom modeling for the JC Penny's Holiday Collection catalogue, circa 1998. JK, it's a studio portrait and we were told to "look natural" and pose this way. At least the feathered bangs have grown out.

At these events, my mother inevitably pivots to introduce me. Her standard introduction includes telling others that this one time, in second grade, I told a kid to back off because, "My mom wears army boots!"

While editing this book, my mom - in full English professor mode - insisted that what I said was, "Oh ya! My mom wore combat boots, and yours didn't!"

Her rationale for this edit is that it sounds more "feisty."

I have no memory of this. It's family lore run amok if you ask me. Or, it's entirely real and I've been repressing the memory.

If anything, someone probably made a "Yo mama" joke - a meme from the 90s, in case you're unfamiliar. Perhaps it was something like, "Yo mama wears army boots." My response to which was probably along the lines of, "Ummm. Yea. She's got a pair. She's kind of particular about keeping them shiny. Why?"

Not very feisty.

How or if this ever even happened, my mom and I agree that hurling a Shakespearean insult would have been so perfect either way. But thinking of the perfect thing to say after the fact is just how life works sometimes.

The spirit of my mom's work has always been about preserving the legacy of the WASP and sharing stories of their boldness, gumption, tenacity, and airborne antics with others. That is also the spirit of this book: To tell a story about remarkable women of service, bravery and patriotism to early readers and future generations of G.I.R.L.s.

The entirety of Natalie J. Stewart-Smith's thesis is available to request from the Smithsonian Libraries Library Catalogue.

Natalie Stewart-Smith and Steve Smith rocking some epic 70s threads, waiting for the city bus at Kimpo Oop outside Camp Eiler.

In the field Ft. Lewis, WA. My mom was the first woman officer to have troop duty in the 9th Infantry Division 1975-76

Swapping flares for formal dress blues. Thanksgiving 1972, Fort McClellan

Additional Resources

If you enjoy this topic, there's a lot of great media and resources where you can learn more about the WASP. Here are a few to consider:

Books

Landdeck, Katherine Sharp. **The Women With Silver Wings: The Inspiring True Story of the Women Airforce Service Pilots of World War II.** New York: Crown, 2020.

Merryman, Molly. **Clipped Wings: The Rise and Fall of the Women Airforce Service Pilots (WASPs) of World War II.** New York University Press, 1998.

Haynsworth, Leslie, and David Toomey. **Amelia Earhart's Daughters: The Wild and Glorious Story of American Women Aviators from World War II to the Dawn of the Space Age.** William Morrow, 1998.

Keil, Sally Van Wagenen. **Those Wonderful Women in Their Flying Machines: The Unknown Heroines of World War II.** New York: Rawson, Wade Publishers, 1979

Rickman, Sarah Byrn. **The Originals: The Women's Auxiliary Ferrying Squadron of World War II**. Disc-Us Books, Inc., 2001.

Streb, Constance. **Women Pilots of World War II.** University of Utah Press, 1991.

Yellin, Emily. **Our Mothers' War: American Women at Home and at the Front During World War II.** Free Press, 2004.

Eder, Mari K. **The Girls Who Stepped Out of Line: Untold Stories of the Women Who Changed the Course of World War II.** Sourcebooks, 2021.

Noggle, Anne. **For God, Country, and the Thrill of It: Women Airforce Service Pilots in World War II.** 1st ed., Texas A&M University Press, 1990.

Granger, Byrd Howell. **On Final Approach: The Women Airforce Service Pilots of W.W. II.** Falconer Publishing Company, 1991.

Media
"Fly Girls." Directed by Laurel Ladevich. PBS, 1999.

"Fifinella - The official mascot of the W.A.S.P." Air Zoo, 2020.
https://www.youtube.com/watch?v=bg55ObylvUA

Historical Collections
National WASP WWII Museum. http://waspmuseum.org/.

Texas Woman's University, WASP Collection.
https://twudigital.contentdm.oclc.org/digital/collection/p214coll2.

Acknowledgments

My dad, Steve Smith. Thank you for your enthusiasm for finding and digitizing the awkward photos of me for this project - perhaps a little too eagerly come to think of it. You have always believed in me...Through every awkward phase, despite every quirk, and I know nothing will change that. Love you, dad.

My husband, Billy Itule. For letting me process out loud, holding space to let me create, and iterate, iterate, iterate. You possess the patience of a saint. It's a miracle and a mystery to me how you show up every single day ready to be the definition of unconditional love for me and our family. You are a truly wonderful man. One-of-a-kind. Irreplaceable. Perfect adjacent. (But don't let that get to your head sweetness!) J'adore you forever.

Lily and Liam. Thank you for wanting me to be an author. Your pride at the very idea is my inspiration. I love you. I love you with all of my heart. I love being your mom. You make our family special, and that will never change. P.S. Please put your laundry away <u>properly</u> and go brush your teeth before the end of this book!

Meggan Hornaday - Teachers are the world's most precious resource and you prove it every day. Your professional perspective, ideas, edits, and encouragement helped me realize my goal of publishing a book. I'll be thankful for forever, and my plan is to be friends just as long. I feel overwhelmingly lucky our own GIRLs are so close. And together, I'm sure you and I will survive them!

My mom, Natalie Stewart-Smith. Thank you for teaching me the definitions of girl and leadership; and for wearing army boots. Minus the footwear, these things are part of me and shape my sense of self and purpose to this day. It's tough to find a greater gift. I'm grateful you put your professor's hat on to edit this book. If you find any mistakes, I owe **you** the quarter this time.

About the Artwork

The 1940s are a stylistically distinct era. From WWII recruiting posters and the Saturday Evening Post to haute couture fashion sketches and mid-century advertising, the look is unmistakable.

Representing the visual identity of the 1940s and the story of the WASPs required a creative process that I like to think Jacqueline Cochran and Nancy Harkness-Love would appreciate. Like the aviation innovations Jackie and Nancy helped pioneer, creating the illustrations in this book with Artificial Intelligence (AI) was test and learn experience.

By giving tools like Midjourney and DALL-E detailed descriptions of subjects, settings, features, mediums, styles, and color palettes, images emerged that I couldn't realize on my own.

I learned so much in the process. Studying images of the WASPs, their flight suits, their uniforms, the planes, their style, and their individual expressions brought me much closer to the women I wanted to tell a story about. At the same time, describing all the nuances in order to build prompts that worked to translate the image in my mind into an illustration I was satisfied with gave me a whole new perspective on what clear direction means!

The results are images that do represent the era, are true to the real-life references, are quite lovely on their own, and work together to tell the story of the WASP. However, it must be said: Seeing the real pictures and artifacts is the best way to experience these G.I.R.L.s. These were real, brave, complex women. I hope these illustrations capture some of that. Most of all, I hope readers of all kinds will want to discover more about the Women Airforce Service Pilots.

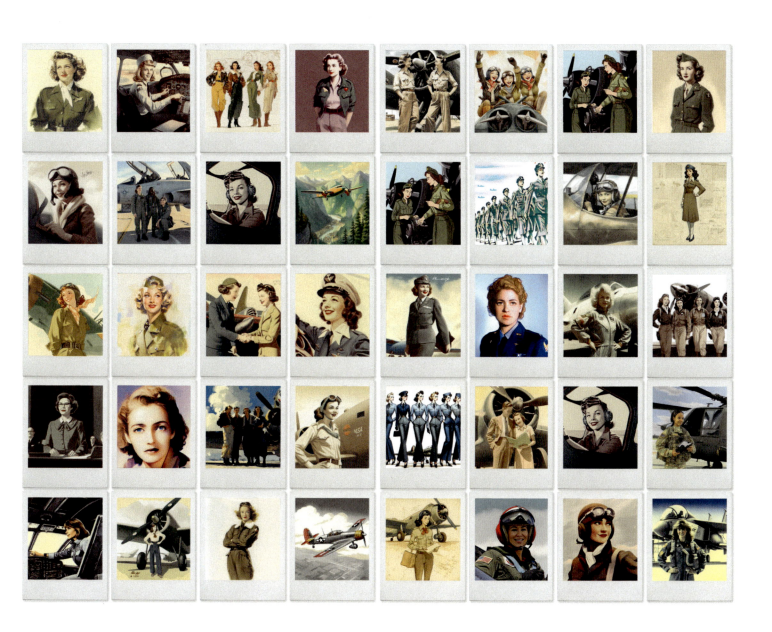

Made in the USA
Monee, IL
28 August 2024

64395838R00024